Greater Than
Pittsburgh
Pennsylvania
USA

50 Travel Tips from a Local

>TOURIST

Patrick Freed

Lock Haven, PA

ISBN: 9781521420331

> TOURIST

BOOK DESCRIPTION

Are you excited about planning your next trip? Do you want to try something new while traveling? Would you like some guidance from a local? If you answered yes to any of these questions, then this book is just for you.

Greater Than a Tourist – Pittsburgh, PA by Patrick Freed offers the inside scope on Pittsburgh, Pennsylvania.

Most travel books tell you how to travel like a tourist. Although there's nothing wrong with that, as a part of the Greater than a Tourist series this book will give you tips and a bunch of ideas from someone who lives at your next travel destination.

In these pages you'll discover local advice that will help you throughout your stay. Greater than a tourist is a series of travel books written by locals.

Travel like a local. Get the inside scope. Slow down, stay in one place, take your time, get to know the people and the culture of a place. Try some things off the beaten path with guidance. Patronize local business and vendors when you travel. Be willing to try something new and have the travel experience of a lifetime.

By the time you finish this book, you will be excited to travel to your next destination. Ten cents of each book purchased is donated to teaching and learning.

CONTENTS

15. Splash Around At The Point

16. Walk Across The Fort Duquesne Bridge

17. Get Immersed In A Movie At The Rangos Omnimax

18. Watch Polar Bears Swim Overhead At The PGH Zoo

19. Listen To Local Musicians

20. Go To Bicycle Heaven

21. Run The Pittsburgh Great Race

22. Become A Paleontologist

23. Go On Top Mt. Washington

24. Hear the Swell of the Pittsburgh Symphony Orchestra

25. Have A Drink At Andy's Wine Bar

26. Take A Trip To Station Square

27. Jam Outdoors At Stage AE

28. Support Local Artists At The Three Rivers Arts Festival

29. Rock A Jersey At A Penguins Game

30. Explore At Carnegie Museum Of Art

31. Take Flight At The Pittsburgh Aviary

32. Grab A Blanket And Catch An Outdoor Movie Showing

33. Walk The Strip District

34. Catch A Show At The Benedum Center

35. Take A Hike In Schenley Park

36. Taste Test At The Market Square Farmer's Market

37. Go Ice Skating In Market Square

38. Stand Inside A Landmark At The Fort Pitt Block House

39. Take A Tour Of The Fort Pitt Museum

40. Speak Your Mind At Steel City Slam

41. Be Part Of A Show At Pittsburgh Public Theater

42. Explore Modern Art At The Mattress Factory

43. Learn About PA Culture At Heinz History Center

44. Become A Photographer At Randyland

45. Drop Your Jaw At The Talent In Heinz Hall

46. Grab Coffee With Friends At Staghorn Garden Cafe

47. Howl At The Moon

48. Walk Up The Pittsburgh Water Steps

49. Eat The Best Burger And Fries At Winghart's

50. Listen To An Audio Tour And Walk The City

> TOURIST

> TOURIST

> TOURIST

Author Bio

Patrick Freed is a student at Slippery Rock University of Pennsylvania, where he is pursuing a Bachelor of Arts degree in English with a focus in creative writing. He also is working toward a minor in French due to his love for the language and culture. He is from a small town just 45 minutes outside of the city of Pittsburgh, Pennsylvania, but considers himself a local because of how frequently he visits the area.

In his free time he enjoys hiking in various Pennsylvania state parks, painting, and going to see musicals and plays at the many theatres in Pittsburgh. This is his first book, which he is thrilled to share with you.

How To Use This Book

This book was written by someone who has lived in an area for over three months. The author has made the best suggestions based on their own experiences in the area. Please check that these places are still available before traveling to the area. Get ready to enjoy your next trip.

WELCOME TO > TOURIST

Introduction

When most outsiders think of Pittsburgh, they think of a city that was once the hub of steel production in the world during the industrial movement, but has since become victim to urban sprawl. However, for those of us who bleed black and gold and only eat our sandwiches and salads with french fries on them, Pittsburgh is so much more. It's a community full of life, culture, and tradition that continues to inspire and touch the hearts of all who pass through the Fort Pitt tunnel.

What sets Pittsburgh apart from other cities is that it doesn't matter how far away you live; if you love the city and all that it stands for, you can call yourself a Pittsburgh native. Whether you live a short 10 minute sprint to downtown or a 30-45 minute drive, you will always be welcomed as a local as you cross the Andy Warhol bridge into the city.

I am on the latter end of that spectrum, growing up in an area that is about a 45 minute drive from downtown, but I have always felt at home in the city. Pittsburgh is packed full of fantastic food, astounding art, and enthusiastic sports fans. You'd be hard pressed to find a group of people who are more proud of where they live than us "yinzers". Us locals have a passion and a great pride for our city and I hope that these tips will help you to see why.

1. *Grab A Bite To Eat At The Original Primanti Bros. Shop*

If a sandwich piled high with freshly sliced deli meat and cheese and topped with crispy french fries, coleslaw, and tomatoes sounds appetizing to you, you have to stop in for a meal at the original Primanti Bros. location. In the early 1930's, during the height of the Great Depression, Joe Primanti made the choice to start selling sandwiches out of a cart to Hungry and hard-working Pittsburghers. Once he realized that he had a successful business going, he took his idea to a storefront in what is known today as the Strip District and nearly 85 years later, people are still enjoying his vision and creation. There's nothing more representative of Pittsburgh, and if you want to explore like a local, you've got to eat like one.

2. Snack Like A Local At Pittsburgh Popcorn Company

When touring the Strip District, you'll quickly come to notice one thing: us Pittsburgh natives know how a thing or two about good food. A local favorite, Pittsburgh Popcorn Co. has a menu that offers every flavor of popcorn from Wisconsin cheddar to sweet caramel kettle corn. If you're interested in a more unique experience, however, they also have a weekly rotation that includes flavors like buffalo wing, thin mint, bacon cheeseburger, and my personal favorite chocolate-peanut butter.

3. See The City From A New Perspective

One of the most popular attractions in Pittsburgh would have to be the Duquesne Incline. Century old cable cars that have been restored for safety and aesthetic purposes will carry you up the hill toward Mt. Washington, an area that provides a scenic overlook of the Pittsburgh skyline. The view offered by the incline is not one to be ignored though. In fact, it has been said that the best way to see the city is through the Duquesne Incline. Though there is really no bad time to go, I think that the best time is after the sun has gone down and the sky is completely dark. The lights of the skyline fill the dark sky and create a picturesque starry scape which can be viewed through the large windows in the cable car.

4. Cheer On The Pittsburgh Pirates At PNC Park

Pittsburghers are serious about their sports, but are especially devoted to the local baseball team; the Pittsburgh Pirates. In the heat of summer, you'd be hard pressed to find a single person not decked out in the team's colors of black and gold. Attending at least one Pirates game is a crucial way to kick off the baseball season. Even if you're not generally a huge sports fan, tickets are relatively cheap, and the arena is a treat in itself. The arena was opened in 2001 and offers a gorgeous view of the famous bright yellow Andy Warhol bridge, scenic skyline, and the glimmering Allegheny River. Cheering on the Pirates is sure to immerse you in Pittsburgh culture and make you feel just like a local.

5. Order The Crab Fries

When attending a Pirates game, there are several traditions you must adhere to in order to make you feel like a true local. One of these is ordering the crab fries from Chickie's and Pete's Crab House and Sports Bar. It is located in section 132 close to third base. Contrary to what you might think, crab fries do not actually contain any crab. Instead, the fries are tossed in Old Bay crab seasoning for a unique and spicy flavor and served with a side of white creamy cheese dip. They might sound pretty average at first, but once you've had them, you too will recognize that they truly are life changing.

6. Root For Your Favorite During The Pierogi Race

Six personified pierogis running around the perimeter of the baseball field may sound a bit odd, but to many Pittsburghers it's a unique tradition that is an important part of the experience of a Pirates game. The pierogis usually come out in-between the fifth and sixth innings and race each other around the outside of the field. It may feel silly to root for a person dressed in a pierogi costume, but trust me, once you see everyone else getting into it, you'll feel even more silly for not doing it.

7. Get Pop Cultured

Pittsburgh is the home of several pop culture icons. Andy Warhol, for example has had a powerful hand in shaping the architecture of the city. The Andy Warhol Museum is located on the North Shore and is dedicated to telling the story of Warhol's life through art and interactive exhibits. The museum also houses the largest collection of Warhol's works. Guests of the museum are invited not only to explore popular pieces created by the artist, but they are also encouraged to experiment with techniques popularized by the artist such as acetate collage and silkscreen printing in the museum's underground studio known as 'The Factory.'

8. Surround Yourself In Nature

In addition to art and urban culture, Pittsburgh also boasts a strong commitment to fostering and preserving nature. Phipp's Conservatory and Botanical Gardens is consistently mentioned in books, magazines, and travel blogs, and once you visit you will see exactly why it has such good reputation. The conservatory houses several varieties of beautiful trees, flowers, and shrubs both native and exotic. Phipp's Conservatory is also known for its approach to teaching about nature. The conservatory hosts several exhibits and events for people of all ages that give them the opportunity to explore, interact, and learn about plants and trees. One other thing that sets Phipp's conservatory apart from other botanical gardens is it's butterfly exhibit. In the spring, the conservatory offers guests the chance to interact with several species of butterflies as they burst free from their cocoons and flutter about the variety of the flowers in the area known as the 'butterfly forest.'

9. Spend The Day At Carnegie Science Center

I, like so many other Pittsburgh-raised children, have fond memories of spending whole days at the Carnegie Science Center. Whether you're traveling with kids or not, the science center offers four floors of interactive scientific fun for all ages. The exhibits are each aimed at educating about different topics such as space science, water systems and natural disasters, and the human body. The easily comprehendible directions and information on each of the different exhibits allows users of all different ages and backgrounds to feel educated and intelligent without feeling intimidated or overwhelmed. My personal favorite experiment to this day is "H2OH!", which offers a comprehensive look at rivers and streams and teaches the importance of conservation of those systems. The exhibit includes fun water themed games that allow guests to splash around in shallow tabletop pools as they learn about how damns are built, the physics of water, and conservation all through a hands-on approach.

10. Experience Breathtaking Architecture

The Cathedral of Learning is located in the Oakland area of Pittsburgh and is part of the University of Pittsburgh. Known locally by students of the university as 'Cathy,' the building houses several departments such as Theatre Arts, English, Religious Studies, and Philosophy. It is also home to a black box theatre and 30 nationality rooms which are each dedicated to celebrating a different culture that helped to make Pittsburgh the great city that it is. The building itself was constructed in 1934 and is comprised of a steel frame that has been covered in Indiana limestone. It celebrates a classical architecture and is considered the second tallest gothic-styled building in the world. Its high ceiling, strong arches, and beautiful steel framework give an ornate and magic atmosphere that will make you feel like you are a student at Hogwarts.

>TOURIST

"Pittsburgh entered the core of my heart when I was a boy and cannot be torn out"

— *Andrew Carnegie*

11. Pay Your Respects To One Of The Greats

Roberto Clemente has been called the greatest baseball player of his time. Not only did he bring the Pittsburgh Pirates to fame, but during his career he also had to endure social injustice and racism. However, he didn't let that phase him. He let his talent speak for itself and let his batting average silence his adversaries. He also dedicated a large portion of his tragically short life to humanitarian work helping underprivileged children. The Roberto Clemente Museum located in the Lawrenceville area in what is known as Engine House 25, and it is devoted to keeping the memory of this amazing athlete and honorable man alive. Through baseball artifacts, art, literature, and memorabilia related to Clemente, the staff of the museum hopes to share the story of the life and times of this magnificent man.

12. Go Kayaking Down The Allegheny River

One of the best ways to see the beautiful Allegheny River that flows through the downtown area is to go kayaking. Kayak Pittsburgh North Shore is a program located right next to PNC park that allows you to rent kayaks for $16.00/hour and sail down the glistening Allegheny. You will get one of the most amazing and unique views of the skyline as you paddle along the water. You can also kayak around the Point at Point State Park , or if you prefer, you can branch off toward the Ohio or Monongahela rivers because the tour is truly self-guided and customizable because of this. It's a great way to cool off on a sunny day in the city and it's also a great way to spend time adventuring with friends and family.

13. Dance The Polka At The Croatian Club

A friend of mine is a member of the Duquesne University Tamburitzan's and has strong ties to her Croatian heritage. One of the most fun times that I've ever had in Pittsburgh was when she brought some friends and me to the Croatian Club. The club serves authentic Croatian food which includes one of the best fried-fish sandwiches I've ever had. The piece of cod was huge, was stacked between a delicious fresh Kaiser roll, and was served with a side of mac n' cheese and traditional Croatian coleslaw. Shortly after dinner commenced, the house band started playing polka music and everyone in the building was encouraged to get up and dance. The atmosphere of the club was cozy and very friendly and the food was inexpensive but high quality. I'd say it's definitely one of the lesser known destinations in Pittsburgh, but it's very worth it.

14. Drive Through The Fort Pitt Tunnel

The Fort Pitt tunnel is a unique piece of architecture that provides an unforgettable experience to its visitors. The dim lights of the tunnel will make you feel like you're on the London Undergound as you're driving. However, once you see the light at the end of the tunnel, the wait will have been well worth it. Once you cross from the tunnel to the bright yellow Andy Warhol bridge, your eyes will be filled with a spectacular view of the Allegheny river and the Pittsburgh skyline. The view is so sought after that it was even included in the film *The Perks of Being a Wallflower.*

15. *Splash Around At The Point*

With its numerous skyscrapers and blacktop streets, it doesn't take very long for Pittsburgh to heat up, and as a tourist, this heat wave can make for a dreadful trip. Luckily, there's one surefire way to cool off while downtown. Point State Park is a beautiful little stretch of green grass and tall trees that provide shade and relaxation on a hot summer day, but the best way to relieve yourself from the heat is to kick off your shoes and dip your feet into the cool water of the Point State Park fountain. You can relax and take some stress away from your feet as you sit next to the cool mist of the fountain and get recharged to continue your trip around the gorgeous city.

16. Walk Across The Fort Duquesne Bridge

Another way to cool off during the heat of the mid-day is to head indoors for a bit. One of my favorite things to do in the city is to watch movies in the IMAX theater located in the Carnegie Science Center. My favorite way to get there is crossing the Fort Duquesne bridge. As you walk along the outside of the bridge, you'll pass by boat landings on the Allegheny, PNC park, and even wildlife. Ducks and geese freely roam the area around the boat docks. The walk takes about 25 minutes and is a great way to get exercise while also getting a nice view of all that the city has to offer.

17. Get Immersed In A Movie At The Rangos Omnimax

Located in the lower level of the Carnegie Science Center, the theater shows a different rotation of movies. The theater even has a concession stand where you can buy slushies, popcorn, candy, and drinks. Tickets are relatively inexpensive (less than $10) and it's a great way to kill an hour during a hot day. However, if you'll be visiting during a colder time of year, such as the Christmas season, the theater is known for showing the film *The Polar Express.* Personally, I feel that it's a great way to get in the Christmas spirit. The surround sound and massive overhead screen create a movie-watching experience that you've never had before and are guaranteed not to forget.

18. Watch Polar Bears Swim Overhead At The PGH Zoo

The Pittsburgh Zoo is home to more than 400 different species and houses 4,000 animals in total. There are several different exhibits and habitats to visit, but the best one by far would have to be the polar bears. If you're lucky, you'll catch them during the time of day where they like to go swimming and you can watch from underneath. The Zoo provides a short tunnel that sits just below the polar bears' pool so you can look through the thick glass and watch as the bears take a dip in the cool water. As you watch through the glass panes, it will feel as if you too are swimming right along with them.

19. Listen To Local Musicians

Each summer, local outdoor venues host what is called the summer concert series. There are about 1-2 concerts per week, all are completely free, and they each give you a taste of the massive amount of talent that's in Pittsburgh. All different kinds of musicians perform, so there truly is something for everyone. Famous acts like The Pittsburgh Symphony and the River City Brass Band will perform as well as smaller, lesser-known performers like The Mavericks and Billy Porter all share the same stage and fill the night with music. Relaxing on the lawn on top of a blanket and listening to music with some friends or a significant other is a great way to spend your summer nights.

20. Go To Bicycle Heaven

You'll quickly come to the understanding that Pittsburgh has some of the most odd museums within its streets. Bicycle Heaven is certainly no exception to this rule. It is the world's largest bicycle museum and bike shop. It is located in the Bellevue area of Pittsburgh and was established in 1996 originally as a bike repair shop, but later rebranded as a museum in 2001. The museum collects and sells vintage bicycle memorabilia as well as new and used bike parts like baskets, seats, and horns. It houses over 4,000 different bikes and collector's items such as themed bikes that include The Beatles and Elvis Presley in addition to other bike related oddities and local artwork. It's a unique museum not to be missed.

>TOURIST

"A good traveler has no fixed plans, and is not intent on arriving."

— *Lao Tzu*

21. Run The Pittsburgh Great Race

If you'll be visiting sometime during September, you should definitely try to sign up for the great race. It's a 5K that is held in the early fall and the course runs through the downtown area and ends in the beautiful Point State Park. The course gives a great tour of the city and as you run, you'll be exposed to all the different types of architecture, including Carlow University and Duquesne University. If you've never ran a 5k before, they're not as intimidating as they sound. The atmosphere is very pleasant and the other runners are very friendly and encouraging. There's no need to worry about timing because all participants are encouraged to run at their own pace.

22. Become A Paleontologist

The Carnegie Museum of Natural History is home to some of the most interesting historical artifacts. the museum is comprised of 3 floors with exhibits that include Native American history, Egyptian history, paleontology, and minerals and gems. A favorite, especially for younger visitors is the "Dinosaurs In Their Time" exhibit. This level of the museum features scientifically accurate recreations of the landscape during the Mesozoic era as well as large dinosaur skeletons. In addition to this display, there is also an interactive exhibit where guests can act like real paleontologists. Guests are invited to strap on a pair of safety goggles, grab a pick and a brush and dig for fossils just like a real paleontologist. While this is primarily aimed at children, I visited the museum not too long ago and no one shamed me for playing in the dirt. You may get a few sideways glances, but excavating your very own "fossil" from the site is a memory that will stick with you no matter your age.

23. Go On Top Mt. Washington

Not only is Mt. Washington home to some of the most expensive and elaborate homes in Pittsburgh, but it also offers landings which provide an amazing overlook of the city. For $0.50, you can use the large binoculars that are provided on each of the landings to look at the city from high above and get a new perspective of the area. If you happen to be around for the fourth of July, I would sincerely recommend that you watch fireworks from Mt. Washington. Bring a couple of foldable chairs with you, ride to the top on the Duquesne Incline and secure your spot. You'll want to make sure to get there early though, because there will be hundreds of other people trying to do the exact same thing as you.

24. Hear the Swell of the Pittsburgh Symphony Orchestra

The Pittsburgh Symphony Orchestra performs several times per year and the style of their performances can vary greatly. They play everything from Tchaikovsky's concertos to symphonic hip hop. The orchestra is made up of several talented musicians who've studied at renowned universities such as Carnegie Mellon and even Juilliard. I've been fortunate enough to see them once and I can vouge for the fact that the experience of the Pittsburgh symphony is deeply beautiful.

25. *Have A Drink At Andy's Wine Bar*

Andy's Wine Bar is the place where Art and Alcohol mix. Not only is the bar named after the famous pop artist and Pittsburgh native Andy Warhol, but the décor of the bar has a modern feel which emulates the late artist. Andy's offers several unique cocktails, a relatively affordable wine selection, and a good selection of beer. In addition to its creative and colorful cocktails, it also is known for its jazz performances which occur every week from Thursday-Saturday. Another cool feature about Andy's Wine Bar is that it's completely free to listen to the Jazz. There is no cover charge of any kind here.

26. Take A Trip To Station Square

Station square is located on the west side of Pittsburgh. It was once the hub of the industrial movement and a place for congregation amongst travelers on the Pittsburgh & Lake Erie Railroad. However, after renovations made in the early 2000's, it is now a premier location for dining and entertainment in the Pittsburgh area. In station square, you will find some of the most unique and trendy shops ever and you will be sure to not leave empty handed. After you're done shopping you can enjoy a nice meal in one of the many restaurants or pubs that the square has. My personal favorite place to eat is Buca Di Beppo, an Italian restaurant that gives huge portions. Each meal is meant to be shared and the whole restaurant is focused around community, so it's a great place to relax with friends and family.

27. Jam Outdoors At Stage AE

This indoor/outdoor venue is located in the heart of downtown right across from Heinz field and PNC Park. The venue is known for hosting independent and lesser-known artists, but sometimes these can be the best concerts to attend. The tickets are relatively cheap and the atmosphere is well worth the price.

28. Support Local Artists At The Three Rivers Arts Festival

The festival is held every summer and lasts about ten days. Each day is packed full of dazzling art, amazing music, and great food. There are booths set up all around The Point and vendors who remain there the whole time, but you'll want to be sure to check the schedule online and find out what unique events will be happening that day. There are always modern art pieces for the artistically and musically inclined, but don't be discouraged, because there are also interactive exhibits all over the place that people of all ages are encouraged to try.

Bonus Tip: Most of the food at the festival will be overpriced because of the convenience of it, but the $3 snow cones next to the National Parks booth are a good investment.

29. Rock A Jersey At A Penguins Game

Known locally as the 'Pens', the Pittsburgh Penguins are the local hockey team. As it was mentioned before, Pittsburghers are serious about their sports. Attending a game at the PPG Paints Arena is one definite way to immerse yourself in this culture. Several nights a week, fans from all over pack into the arena to cheer on the Pens. The building itself is beautiful and outside of the ice rink, you will find all kinds of vendors trying to sell you everything from pretzels and bottled water to life insurance or a credit card. If you're going to attend, definitely make sure that you purchase some sort of Penguins related merch or at the very least deck yourself out head to toe in black and gold, because you do not want to be caught in the opposing team's colors.

30. Explore At Carnegie Museum Of Art

The Carnegie Museum of Art houses several diverse types of artworks. I would definitely recommend taking a tour if possible. The museum is laid out so that as you look at each painting, you are doing so in a chronological order. What I mean is the wings of the museum are broken up into periods, such as impressionism, cubism, etc. The tour will begin with a very classic form of painting with no visible paint strokes and will then move on to impressionist paintings, such as those created by Van Gogh and Claude Monet. From there, you will be lead to view several other forms of art such as ornate ironwork and sculptures. The whole time, you will be encouraged to think critically about each piece and examine the physical and emotional differences between the various styles of art.

>TOURIST

"The three most beautiful cities in the world are Paris; St. Petersburg, Russia; and Pittsburgh. If Pittsburgh were situated somewhere in the heart of Europe, tourists would eagerly journey hundreds of miles out of their way to visit it. Its setting is spectacular."

— Brendan Gill

31. Take Flight At The Pittsburgh Aviary

The National Aviary, located in Pittsburgh is the largest in the world with over 500 birds and over 150 different species. The aviary is a great place to educate yourself about the importance of species diversity in a fun and interactive way. The staff of the aviary also has a strong commitment to teaching the importance of conservation. They run several projects that attempt to engage the public in their effort to preserve wildlife.

32. Grab A Blanket And Catch An Outdoor Movie Showing

Every summer from June until August, different parks in the Pittsburgh area host outdoor movie screenings. After the sun has gone down and the sky gets dark is when the movies start. They show all different kinds of movies ranging from kid-friendly movies like *Finding Dory* to action packed flicks like *Rogue One* and classics that everyone can enjoy like *Ghostbusters*. Bring some blankets, pillows, and some snacks and come to one of Pittsburgh's beautiful parks for a fun night out.

33. Walk The Strip District

The strip district is located along the Allegheny river and spans from 11th to 33rd street. With its several vendors, it's a great place to do some light grocery shopping, sample exotic foods, or even just take a nice stroll. The strip offers many different stores and sells everything from smoked meats to baby clothes. It's essentially the Pittsburgh version of China Town, but with better food. A personal favorite place of mine to go when I am touring with the Strip District would have to be Pittsburgh Popcorn Company. The sweet aroma that wafts out from there is one that simply cannot be passed up.

34. Catch A Show At The Benedum Center

The Benedum Center is a gorgeous theatre located in the heart of the Cultural District in downtown Pittsburgh. Each season, it is the stage of choice for several different musicians, dancers, and performers. Every year, The Benedum hosts the Pittsburgh Ballet Theatre as they perform the Nutcracker. I spend a good amount of my time hanging out in the cultural district and I have seen several musicals in the theater, so you can trust me when I say that it is a beautiful location. The theater is large enough to accommodate a substantial audience, but small enough so that it still feels like a rather intimate atmosphere. Some of the best shows I've ever seen have been at The Benedum.

35. Take A Hike In Schenley Park

If you're looking to get out of the heat and stress of the city for a while, Schenley Park is the place for you. The park is a gorgeous stretch of just over 450 acres that holds tons of beautiful and scenic hiking, walking, and biking trails as well as a swimming pool and playgrounds. The trails are far enough away so that you won't have to be caught up in the sounds of the city, but can instead enjoy a moment of peace in nature.

36. Taste Test At The Market Square Farmer's Market

Every Thursday from 10:00 AM – 2:00 PM, over 30 vendors fill the area of market square selling everything from fresh home-grown fruits and vegetables to locally-made home décor. The farmer's market is a great way to spend your morning sampling all different kinds of foods and meeting new people. There is also a free concert in the afternoon from the hours of 11:30 – 1:30 which gives a nice break from the sounds of traffic in the city. One thing you have to do is find the vendor who sells locally-made gelato and sample some of their creations. The pineapple-jalapeno was my favorite because it was sweet with a spicy kick on the end, but they also sell flavors like vanilla, chocolate, lavender, etc.

37. Go Ice Skating In Market Square

If you'll be around from the months of December – mid-February, another great activity you can do is go ice skating in Market square. Every winter, the center of market square becomes marked off and gets an ice rink put into it, and in the center of the rink is an enormous Christmas tree decked out in thousands of colorful bulbs and lights. If you get the opportunity to go skating here around Christmas time, you should absolutely go for it, because it is a truly magical experience.

38. Stand Inside A Landmark At The Fort Pitt Block House

The Fort Pitt Block House is all that remains of the army base known as Fort Pitt that was used during the French and Indian War. It has been standing strong for approximately 250 years and continues to be a reminder of our nation's past. The interior of the block house is just as it would have been during the time of its original use with the exception of historical artifacts that have been added to make it a sought after tourist destination and to teach guests about its history.

39. Take A Tour Of The Fort Pitt Museum

If after visiting the Fort Pitt Blockhouse, you're eager to learn more about the history behind it, head on over to the Fort Pitt Museum. It's located in Point State Park, just across from the blockhouse and is dedicated to educating its visitors on the French and Indian War and the important role that Pittsburgh had in it. The museum is made up of two floors, both containing equally interesting historical artifacts and artwork that was inspired by this war. Admission to the museum is cheap, which also makes it a great way to get out of the sun for a little bit if you find yourself touring on a particularly hot day.

40. Speak Your Mind At Steel City Slam

Every Tuesday a group of talented poets and thinkers meet up at Capri's Pizzeria and Bar, which is located in East Liberty, for a night of slam poetry guaranteed to take you for an emotional trip. Anyone who is prepared with three poems that can be read in three minutes or less is welcome to participate, however, no one is required to. There are several things you can do when attending a slam. If you wish, you may judge the poets who are reading. Simply ask the host when you enter. If you're not up for that, listening to the amazing talent that pours out from Pittsburghers is enjoyable in itself. I recommend grabbing a couple friends, ordering a delicious pepperoni pizza, and enjoying what the poets have to offer. The atmosphere of the slam is very inviting and the people there will be glad to have you.

\>TOURIST

"This is the only city in America with an entrance. You slide and slither into most downtowns, passing through gradual layers of even more intensely built-up sprawl, and you do not so much enter the center as realize after you are there that it is all around you. Not Pittsburgh. Pittsburgh is entered with glory and drama."

— Paul Goldberger

41. Be Part Of A Show At Pittsburgh Public Theater

The intimate seating arrangement of the Pittsburgh Public Theater makes for an unforgettable performance. The theater puts on several shows per season and they range from wacky plays by up and coming playwrights to well established musicals. One thing is certain though; you will not forget your experience in this theater. Some seats are so close that the performers may try to incorporate you into the show, and some are literally on the stage, so you won't have much of a choice but to become a part of it. I saw the musical *My Fair Lady* at this theater a few years ago and I was amazed at the theatricality that the show was able to convey for it being such a small space. Pittsburgh Public shows are unique and sure to be one of your favorites.

42. Explore Modern Art At The Mattress Factory

The Mattress Factory is a modern art museum that gets its name from the building's original purpose. The building was once a mattress factory, but after being abandoned, Barbara Luderowski decided to purchase the property and turn it into a community for art and artists. Since its opening in the late 1970's, the Mattress Factory has seen numerous art installations come through its walls. The museum is made up of three floors and each floor contains many interesting and thought provoking exhibits. There are permanent installations as well as a rotation of temporary installations. My favorite installation would have to be "Pleiades" by James Turrell. It really changes your perspective both literally and figuratively and gives you an opportunity to think critically.

43. Learn About PA Culture At Heinz History Center

The Heinz History Center is Pennsylvania's largest history museum and is affiliated with the Smithsonian Institution. The museum is especially interesting because its dedicated to teaching the culture and history of the local area. That means that when you enter the museum, you will literally be a part of history. The museum is located in the historic Strip district and has exhibits that are dedicated to topics such as Pittsburgh sports, the life and times of beloved Pittsburgh native and T.V. personality Mr. Rodgers, and the history of the industries which put Pittsburgh on the global map.

44. Become A Photographer At Randyland

Located in the Northside, Randyland is actually the home of artist Randy Gilson. He bought the property in the '90s after falling in love with the neighborhood. The area was not the nicest place to live and had a bad reputation for being a "rough" neighborhood. Gilson decided to spend what little money he had saved and clean up the neighborhood and turn his home into the magnificent piece of art that it is today. Randyland is a colorful and eclectic piece of architecture that has bright colored paint and vibrant plants spilling from every corner. Admission to tour his home is completely free and photography is encouraged. Randy's hard work to renovate the home really shines and makes for a gorgeous and colorful backdrop for your next selfie.

45. Drop Your Jaw At The Talent In Heinz Hall

Heinz Hall is another of the gorgeous theaters that Pittsburgh has to offer. The theater is considerably larger than The Benedum and it is the home of the famous Pittsburgh Symphony Orchestra. The stage also is set to see the talent of other famous musicians such as Idina Menzel and the cast of the stage musical "An American in Paris" in it's 2017-2018 season. I've been lucky enough to have seen a couple different shows in Heinz Hall and I can attest to the fact that it is a beautiful and luxurious theatre and it will provide a musical experience that will stay with you.

46. Grab Coffee With Friends At Staghorn Garden Cafe

Staghorn Café is one of the most unique places in the city. It offers what you would expect find in a coffee shop, such as lattes, cappuccinos, cold brews, iced coffees, etc. However, it also offers homemade baked goods like bagels, scones, and muffins. The café is also known as a place to find oddities like unique homegoods, gardening tools, and locally-made goods. The atmosphere is relaxing and inviting, making it the perfect place to chat the day away with close friends.

47. Howl At The Moon

Howl at the Moon is a dueling piano bar located in downtown Pittsburgh. To enter the bar, there is a $5 cover charge due to the live entertainment that is present. The drinks are reasonably priced and the atmosphere makes for a great night out. The musicians are quite talented and play popular hits that pretty much everyone can enjoy. It can tend to get a bit too noisy as it is packed with 20 somethings, but the music and vibe will make your trip worth it.

48. Walk Up The Pittsburgh Water Steps

The Pittsburgh water steps are a part of the North Shore Riverfront Park and are a great way to cool off and relieve some stress during a hot day of touring. The steps are located next to PNC park and as the water cascades over the steps in a fountain like motion, it creates a peaceful sound that distracts from the noise of the nearby baseball field. The water steps are a fun place to splash around for people of all ages, so kick your shoes off and enjoy some cool refreshing water.

49. Eat The Best Burger And Fries At Winghart's

Winghart's Burger and Whiskey Bar is located in Market Square. The restaurant is small and intimate, but if you're looking for some more space, I would definitely recommend eating on the patio. The patio seats are the perfect place to enjoy your meal and a lovely view of the square. Winghart's is known for its insanely unique food combinations, but what's even more appealing about this place is that nearly everything is sourced locally and made in-house. They have a strong commitment to knowing where their food comes from and making sure that the customer can be aware of this as well. Any of their interesting french fry combinations is definitely worth ordering, but I would be doing you disservice if I didn't tell you to order the Loaded Baked Potato fries. They come smothered in fresh sharp cheddar and topped with bacon, sour cream, and chives. If you're not full enough after eating those, I would also recommend the Carson Street chicken burger. Smothered in pepperjack cheese and topped with caramelized onions, bacon, spinach, and a garlic aioli, it's unlike anything you've ever tasted.

50. Listen To An Audio Tour And Walk The City

If you're someone who's looking to explore a new city, but is worried about not having a planned itinerary, the Walking Tour of Pittsburgh might be the way to go. Students and faculty of Robert Morris University worked together to create a one-hour walking tour of the city that will give you information about Pittsburgh's past, the architecture behind the city, and other details about what makes Pittsburgh so great. You will also be given the opportunity to have a coffee in the shop where the beans are roasted or enjoy one the famous sandwiches loaded with french fries that the city is known for. All you have to do take the tour is log onto the university's website and search for the walking tour. From there, just download the audio file, print off a map, and you'll be on your way to exploring the city like a true local.

>TOURIST

> TOURIST

Please read other Greater than a Tourist Books.

Join the >Tourist Mailing List :
http://eepurl.com/cxspyf

Facebook:
https://www.facebook.com/GreaterThanATourist

Pinterest:
http://pinterest.com/GreaterThanATourist

Instagram:
http://Instagram.com/GreaterThanATourist

> TOURIST

Greater than a Tourist

Please leave your honest review of this book on Amazon and Goodreads. Thank you.

> TOURIST
Greater than a Tourist

You can find Greater Than a Tourist books on Amazon.

>TOURIST

>TOURIST

>TOURIST

Made in the USA
San Bernardino, CA
23 August 2017